D1716983

THE LIFE CYCLE OF A

Turtle

By Colleen Sexton

BELLWETHER MEDIA · MINNEAPOLIS, MN

Note to Librarians, Teachers, and Parents:

Blastoff! Readers are carefully developed by literacy experts and combine standards-based content with developmentally appropriate text.

Level 1 provides the most support through repetition of high-frequency words, light text, predictable sentence patterns, and strong visual support.

Level 2 offers early readers a bit more challenge through varied simple sentences, increased text load, and less repetition of high-frequency words.

Level 3 advances early-fluent readers toward fluency through increased text and concept load, less reliance on visuals, longer sentences, and more literary language.

Level 4 builds reading stamina by providing more text per page, increased use of punctuation, greater variation in sentence patterns, and increasingly challenging vocabulary.

Level 5 encourages children to move from "learning to read" to "reading to learn" by providing even more text, varied writing styles, and less familiar topics.

Whichever book is right for your reader, Blastoff! Readers are the perfect books to build confidence and encourage a love of reading that will last a lifetime!

This edition first published in 2011 by Bellwether Media, Inc.

No part of this publication may be reproduced in whole or in part without written permission of the publisher. For information regarding permission, write to Bellwether Media, Inc., Attention: Permissions Department, 5357 Penn Avenue South, Minneapolis, MN 55419.

Library of Congress Cataloging-in-Publication Data
Sexton, Colleen A., 1967–
The life cycle of a turtle / by Colleen Sexton.
    p. cm. — (Blastoff! readers. Life cycles)
    Summary: "Developed by literacy experts for students in grades kindergarten through three, this book follows turtles as they transform from eggs to adults. Through leveled text and related images, young readers will watch these creatures grow through every stage of life"—Provided by publisher.
    Includes bibliographical references and index.
    ISBN 978-1-60014-452-3 (hardcover : alk. paper)
    1. Turtles–Life cycles–Juvenile literature. I. Title.
    QL666.C5S49 2010
    597.92–dc22   2010000707

Printed in the United States of America, North Mankato, MN.
080110   1162

Contents

Introducing Turtles!   4

The Egg Stage   9

The Hatchling Stage   16

The Adult Stage   20

Glossary   22

To Learn More   23

Index   24

Turtles are slow-moving **reptiles**. They live on land, near fresh water, and in the ocean.

box turtle

snapping turtle

sea turtle

painted turtle

There are about 250 kinds of turtles. The smallest is 4 inches (10 centimeters) long. The largest is 8 feet (2.4 meters) long.

Turtles have shells to protect their bodies. Most turtles can pull their heads, legs, and tails inside their shells when they sense danger.

Turtles grow and change in stages.
The stages of a turtle's **life cycle**
are egg, hatchling, and adult.

adult

egg

hatchling

A male turtle **courts** a female turtle. He might sway and bob his head. The turtles might touch each other's faces or smell each other's tails.

The male and female **mate**. The female is ready to lay eggs a few months later.

The female turtle digs a nest with her back legs. The nest will help protect the eggs from raccoons, foxes, and other **predators**.

The female lays her eggs in the nest and covers them. Some kinds of turtles lay only one egg. Others lay 100 eggs or more!

The nest of eggs is called a **clutch**.
Most turtle eggs are soft. They can
be round or oval.

Baby turtles grow inside the eggs for about two to three months. Then they are ready to **hatch**!

Female turtles often
hatch from eggs kept
in a warm nest. A cool
nest often produces
male turtles.

Each baby turtle uses a sharp **egg tooth** to break out of its egg shell.

egg tooth

Newly hatched turtles are called hatchlings. The hatchlings push and dig their way out of the nest.

Then they scurry away from the nest to hide from predators.

Each hatchling will grow up on its own.
A hatchling is small and weak. It must
find food and stay safe.

Turtles do most of their growing during the first five to ten years of their lives.

After ten years, turtles grow more slowly. They can live a long time. Some kinds of turtles live 150 years or more!

Most turtles are ready to mate when they are 2 to 20 years old. Each egg a female lays is the start of a new life cycle!

Glossary

clutch—a group of eggs laid at the same time in the same place

courts—moves in a way to attract a mate; male turtles move their heads or bodies to court female turtles.

egg tooth—a sharp, hard point of skin near the tip of a baby turtle's nose; the egg tooth falls off a few days after the baby turtle hatches.

hatch—to break out of an egg

life cycle—the stages of life of an animal; a life cycle includes being born, growing up, having young, and dying.

mate—to join together to produce young

predators—animals that hunt and eat other animals

reptiles—cold-blooded animals that have a backbone and lay eggs to produce young

To Learn More

AT THE LIBRARY

Curtis, Jennifer Keats. *Turtles In My Sandbox*. Mount Pleasant, S.C.: Sylvan Dell, 2006.

Franks, Katie. *Turtles Up Close*. New York, N.Y.: PowerKids Press, 2008.

Hipp, Andrew. *The Life Cycle of a Painted Turtle*. New York, N.Y.: PowerKids Press, 2002.

ON THE WEB

Learning more about life cycles is as easy as 1, 2, 3.

1. Go to www.factsurfer.com.

2. Enter "life cycles" into the search box.

3. Click the "Surf" button and you will see a list of related Web sites.

With factsurfer.com, finding more information is just a click away.

Index

adult, 7

clutch, 12

danger, 6

egg, 7, 9, 10, 11, 12, 13, 14, 21

egg shell, 15

egg tooth, 15

female turtle, 8, 9, 10, 11, 14, 21

food, 18

growing, 7, 13 ,18, 19, 20

hatching, 13, 14, 16

hatchling, 7, 16, 18

life cycle, 7, 21

male turtle, 8, 9, 14

mating, 9, 21

nest, 10, 11, 12, 14, 16, 17

predators, 10, 17

reptiles, 4

shell, 6

size, 5

The images in this book are reproduced through the courtesy of: Robert Ranson, front cover; Richard J. Green/Photo Researchers, Inc., front cover (egg), pp. 7 (egg), 13 (small); Jack Goldfarb/Photolibrary, front cover (hatchling), pp. 7 (hatchling), 19; Constance McGuire, front cover (adult), pp. 6, 7 (adult); Juniors Bildarchiv/Photolibrary, pp. 4-5, 14 (small); Carol Heesen, p. 5 (snapping turtle); Rich Carey, p. 5 (sea turtle); Jody Dingle, p. 5 (painted turtle); Juniors Bildarchiv, pp. 8-9, 9 (small), 12-13, 21; Philippe Henry/Photolibrary, p. 10; Joe McDonald/Animals Animals – Earth Scenes, p. 11; Lynn M. Stone/naturepl.com, pp. 14-15; Suzanne L. & Joseph T. Collins/Photo Researchers, Inc., pp. 16-17; Michael Francis/Animals Animals – Earth Scenes, p. 18; ARCO/H. Reinhard/Age Fotostock, p. 20.